Table of Contents

Introduction

Disclaimer: I am not a flight instructor. The information in this book should not be used as a substitute for actual flight training. The advice I relate in this book should only be viewed as information to help support and enhance your flight school experience.

Like many people, you may have an interest in aviation and have told yourself that you will get your pilot's license ... someday. Thanks to this book, you can make your aviation dreams a reality!

The purpose of this book is to serve as a guide to help any new flight student help make the most of their experience. This book helps flight students plan and organize a strategy to get a private pilots' license. The goal of this book is to help students maximize the value of their time and money and take the steps needed to create the best and least stressful outcome possible. This book discusses requirements to become a pilot in both the United States and Canada, so aspiring pilots in both countries can both benefit from the insights in this book.

This book is meant to benefit anyone who wishes to gain the insights of an actual, private pilot. The information in this book is the stuff that I wish someone would have told me before I began flight school. I wrote this book to help make it easier for others to complete their flight school training with the best outcome possible.

As a private pilot myself, I hope to share my trials and tribulations, and the things I learned along the way on this journey. In writing this book, I hope to help anyone seeking their pilots' license in the safest, easiest, most cost-effective, and most enjoyable way possible.

Chapter 1: My Story (foreward)

Thinking about learning to fly brings up a host of emotions from nostalgia, to frustration, and finally, to triumph and pride. I had wanted to learn to fly since I was ten years old, when I would often go flying with my father – a private pilot and airplane salesman. The sense of wonder and exhilaration that flying inspired in me stuck with me throughout my life.

Unfortunately, that sense of wonder and exhilaration was matched by an equally powerful sense of the daunting challenge of actually learning to fly. I didn't want to have to sit around reading instruction books, studying for exams, and practicing in my chair at home – I wanted to get off the ground and pilot a real plane!

To my mother's relief I decided to turn down the opportunity to fly for free with the Air Cadets (she was not excited about the prospect of her ten-year-old son flying a plane thousands of feet above the ground). This is a decision I regret to this day.

. . .

As an adult, carrying with me both the excitement and passion to fly and the regret at not having taken the opportunity when I was younger, I committed myself wholeheartedly to becoming a pilot. Nothing was going to keep me from soaring the skies in a plane that I was piloting!

I made the unflinching decision to attend flight school. I enrolled in the only flight school near my home. Even with my intense dedication, powerful motivation, and strong sense of self-discipline, I still ran into what seemed like every conceivable challenge (and some that I wouldn't have guessed in a thousand years).

I write this guide to save you from the trials and tribulations – not to mention costs in time and money – that I experienced in flight school. It's hard to express the frustration I experienced from the challenges I was thrust into in flight school. A major source of my frustration was my experience with my flight instructor – or, I should say, instructors (as in multiple).

During my time in flight school I was passed around from instructor to instructor so many times I felt like there was a bet going with the flight school administration to see how many instructors they could assign to me. My instructors handed me off so many times there was a section of training that I ended up having to repeat eight times before I could get through it uninterrupted. I even had one instructor who became so aggressive that he actually lashed out at me physically while I was landing! ("Unpleasurable" is a serious understatement of my experience with this flight school.)

Every time I switched instructors, I would unknowingly acquire a new knowledge gap between what my last instructor was teaching me and what my new instructor wanted to dive into. Of course, I couldn't know what I was missing, because I wasn't aware of the information I wasn't learning!

As a result of these knowledge gaps, I ended up having to repeat the entire ground school syllabus as well as the flight test readiness assessments. Needless to say, this was a monumental waste of my time and money.

Beyond the man-made issues I faced from the flight school, I had to contend with Toronto's temperate climate and the difficulties this presented for flying. This made solo flights a real struggle. Not only did I have to waste time waiting for agreeable weather, but I had to waste money on instructor-led flights while I was waiting so I didn't lose all the knowledge and currency I had gained by the time I actually got into the air for my solo! (Not to mention the emotional energy wasted coping with the politics and poor teaching management at my flight school.)

. . .

(Phew. What a mess, huh? I know after reading all of this you are probably wondering why I didn't just throw in the towel and devote my energy to something less stressful like learning to be a heart surgeon. The fact that I didn't is a testament to the unflappable power of the drive to get into the air as a pilot. None of this is meant to discourage you from taking up flight lessons. Quite the opposite, this story should be taken as an example of some of the (albeit more unlikely) issues that can arise and a warning to make sure you get your ducks in a row before enrolling. This way you can make sure that you get the most out of what should – and what, for me, ended up being – a wonderful, exhilarating, life-changing experience.)

. . .

Then it finally happened! The fates smiled on me and I found the first instructor that I felt justified in actually calling a "teacher". Not just someone with more knowledge than me who was simply present, but a mentor, someone to impart their knowledge and who was engaged in the experience, not just physically present. We clicked right away. He cared about seeing me succeed. He guided me in my journey to learn how to take flight instead of just shoving me off my perch and watching me flap around. He challenged me in a way that made sense to me and helped me grow but still made learning to fly a safe and enjoyable experience.

Not only did my flight mentor excel at teaching me the parts of the course that he was assigned, but he went the extra mile with me and help me not merely complete but excel in all of my flight school studies. To this day I still thank him for being such a wonderful teacher and for the pivotal role he played in helping me realize my dreams to sail the skies. Thank you, Paris sir!

I am also thankful that I filmed my entire flight student experience as well as my final flight. Looking back on the journey that has led me to where I am fills me with a satisfaction that is hard to express until you have been there.

. . .

As a child, I dreamt of soaring through the air, maneuvering the skies in a metal bird – an extension of me through my seat in the pilot's chair. However, I placed this dream on the backburner for years. Later, as an adult I endured a long, strenuous journey in mission to realize this dream. My zeal and determination carried me through those struggles and helped me endure until I found someone who would not only facilitate but inspire my learning. Now that I have achieved this lifelong dream, I feel a joyful airiness and a distinct confidence.

The trials and tribulations were NOT necessary aspects of this journey, if I had known how to I would have avoided them and would not have lost anything in the process. Flying is an amazing experience, it should shore up exhilaration, wonder, and ambition, not frustration. This is my hope for you in reading this guide: to learn from my experiences and make this aviation journey as fulfilling and enjoyable as possible.

Good luck and enjoy this rare and precious journey to the skies!

CHAPTER 2

According to the Federal Aviation Administration's U.S. Civil Airmen Statistics for 2019, about 664,565 Americans hold a pilot license (0.002% of the US population). According to Transport Canada, for 2008 (the most recent data), 47,369 Canadians hold an airplane pilot's license (0.0012% of the Canadian population).

Congratulations on deciding to pursue a dream that few people will experience firsthand! Get excited, curious, and meticulous. Be ready to learn all you can. Once you get hooked on flying, it may change how you define yourself.

At the beginning of this journey, it's important to ask yourself some basic questions. Checking in with yourself will help you better understand your motivations for becoming a pilot and help you figure out your flying goals. Questions you should be thinking about include:

- **Why do I want to become a pilot?** There are many good reasons to become a pilot. You can be a private pilot, a person who flies for fun, a commercial pilot, even a military pilot.
- **What do I want aviation to do for me?** Think about whether you wish to fly for fun, income, or both.

Whatever your answer to these questions, make sure you answer them honestly. That's why the genuine answers to these questions will determine the direction of your aviation career. They will also help guide your approach and treatment of the information in this book.

2.1 CANADIAN AND US PILOT RATINGS

Other than exam requirements, which are discussed in the next section, the following overview will provide you with an overview of pilot license ratings in Canada and the US and a general idea of the kind of general and flight training requirements for each pilot license rating. The lowest level is the student pilot certificate, which has the least amount of privilege but can help you get the training you need to get a more advanced certification. Other types of flying certificates with more privilege can also be granted for recreational, private, commercial, or airline pilots. So, for example, you can obtain a student pilot certificate, complete flight school, and then apply for a private pilot's license.

Canadian Pilot License Ratings

In Canada, per Transport Canada regulations, the first rating - or level - of flight licensing is the Recreational Pilot Permit. This requires you to be 16 years old and have completed 25 hours of flight training. It does not require ground school but does require that you have passed the Transport Canada flight and written exams. If you only have a recreational pilot license you will have to abide by certain restrictions. You will only be able to carry one passenger and you will only be able to fly planes with a maximum of four seats.

The next rating in Canada is the Private Pilot License (PPL). You must be 17 years old and have completed a minimum of 45 hours of flight training. This rating does require that you have completed at least 40 hours of ground school and also requires that you have passed the flight and written exams.

Once you have obtained your Private Pilot License you can begin to gain endorsement ratings such as Night Flying which requires a minimum of 10 hours of night flying training including 2 hours of cross-country and 5 hours of solo flying.

After this rating is the Commercial Pilot License. This requires that you be 18 years old and have completed 200 hours of flight time with 100 hours of Pilot in Command time and 20 hours of cross-country time.

US Pilot License Ratings

In the US, per Federal Aviation Administration (FAA) regulations, the first Pilot License rating is the Private Pilot License (PPL). This requires that you be 17 years old and have completed a minimum of 40 hours of flying time including 20 hours with a flight instructor. As well as 3 hours of cross country, 3 hours of night flying, 3 hours using flight instruments and 10 hours of solo flight times including 5 hours of cross country.

Obtainment of an instrument rating allows you to fly in inclement weather (using only flight instruments rather than external visuals). You must already hold a PPL to obtain this rating. You must also complete 50 hours of cross country flight time as Pilot in Command and 40 hours of real or simulated instrument flying. Finally, you must also complete 15 hours of instrument flight training from an instructor.

The last rating is the Commercial Pilot Certificate. This license can be co-validated internationally. You must be 18 years old and hold a PPL to obtain a Commercial Pilot Certificate. You must also complete 250 hours of flight time including 100 hours in powered aircraft and 50 hours in airplanes. As well as 100 hours of Pilot in Command time (50 of these hours in an airplane), 50 hours of cross-country time (10 in an airplane), 10 hours of instrument training, 10 hours of complex training, and 10 hours of solo training.

2.2 Once You Have Decided You Want to Fly: Complete the Medical & Written Exams

Before you decide to dive into flight school, the first step is to complete a medical exam from an aviation medical examiner. Beyond the general medical clearance needed to fly, different pilot license ratings and endorsements require different levels of medical clearance. You can find an aviation medical examiner through a Google search or by asking the instructors or administrators at a local flight school. Flight training is a huge investment. Before you earmark - or spend - your time and money learning to fly, you need to learn what level of medical clearance you are eligible for.

First, you should get your required medical endorsement from an aviation physician. This will tell you if earning your license as a pilot is possible before you invest your time and money.

The written exams you need to take depend on whether you live in the United States or Canada. In the United States, people who wish to pilot an aircraft must obtain certification from the Federal Aviation Administration (FAA). An FAA-issued pilot certificate means that you are legally authorized to act as the pilot-in-command of an aircraft.

The first step you need to take to work towards getting your pilot's license is to get the written exams out of the way. This is also the most important step; without your pilot's license, you will not be able to fly a plane, which will delay most of the other steps in this process.

The academic syllabus for flight school is made up of four areas: Navigation, Meteorology, Air Law, and Aeronautics. If you don't have a science and math background, your focus must be on Navigation and Meteorology since they are the most complicated academic components.

In general, you will need to complete a certification to be able to fly, whether as a student or a private pilot. The student pilot license (or "permit" in Canada) acts as a piloting "learner's permit" – this will be the first license that you will want to obtain, though you do not need to be licensed to take aviation lessons.

Both the US and Canada require a pilot's license before you can command an aircraft privately — that is, not for pay. The licensing requirements are determined by the International Civil Aviation Organization (ICAO), but their implementation is different from country to country.

The PPL (Private Pilot's License) Exam

A private pilot's license or PPL is a type of pilot license that allows the holder to act as pilot in command of an aircraft privately. The license requirements are determined by the International Civil Aviation Organization (ICAO), but implementation varies widely from country to country. According to the ICAO, it is obtained by successfully completing a course with at least 40 hours (45 in Europe) of flight time, passing seven written exams, completing a solo cross-country flight (the minimum cumulative solo flight time is 10 hours), and successfully demonstrating flying skills to an examiner during a flight test (including an oral exam).

Written Pilot Plot Exams in the United States

FAA pilot certificates do not expire, though they are a privilege and can be revoked or suspended by the FAA. It's important to know that a pilot must maintain what is called *currency* — by having recent flight experience relevant to the type(s) of piloting undertaken.

Written Pilot Exams in Canada

All pilots and flight crew members must obtain a permit or license from the Canadian government before flying. In Canada, pilot licenses are administered by Transport Canada in accordance with the Aeronautics Act and the Canadian Aviation Regulations. Pilots operating Canadian-registered aircraft or act as a flight crew member in Canada with a license or permit issued by Transport Canada.

For Canadians, we recommend online ground school at Harv's Air (www.harvsair.com). The exams you will need to take include the private pilot's license (PPL) exam and the PSTAR.

Private Pilot License (PPL) — Aeroplane

The Private Pilot License or PPL — Aeroplane allows the holder to pilot an airplane. This is the most commonly held license in Canada and is the first license that you must earn to become a pilot. Once you obtain this license, you can conduct day flying of single-engine non-high-performance airplanes in accordance with VFR, unless you obtain other ratings, such as seaplane, multi-engine, multi-engine centerline thrust, night, VFR-Over-the-Top, and/or instrument ratings.

Transport Canada Pre Solo Test of Air (PSTAR)

The PSTAR exam is designed to test the student pilot's knowledge of Air Regulations and Air Traffic Control Procedures. The PSTAR exam, therefore, ensures that the student has the required knowledge of the necessary Canadian Aviation Regulations and the Aeronautical Information Manual before flying without their instructor. A grade of 90% is required to pass the PSTAR.

It's a good idea to enlist the help of your flight school in this process. They have the most up-to-date knowledge of the tests you would need to complete. You can ask your flight school to start a student file for you and for any quizzes that they require to be completed. Then, you can work towards preparing for and passing the required exams.

The PSTAR exam, originally called the Pre-Solo Test of Air Regulations, is - as the title suggests - focused on air regulations and procedures and includes questions covering 14 components:

- Collision Avoidance
- Visual Signals
- Communications
- Aerodromes and Airports
- Equipment
- Pilot Responsibilities
- Wake Turbulence
- Aero Medical
- Flight Plans and Flight Itineraries
- Clearances and Instructions
- Aircraft Operations
- General Airspace
- Controlled Airspace
- Aviation Occurrence

Principal Air offers a comprehensive and user-friendly PSTAR Exam prep guide.

Air Law is a key component of piloting exams and studying for this part of the exam will likely represent a bulk of your study time as there are a significant amount of air laws pertaining to different topics and circumstances such as navigation, air traffic, flying near aerodromes, and more. Further, this is one of the most difficult parts of the exam, not only because of the breadth of topics covered but also because a large amount of knowledge required to pass this part of the PSTAR or pilot exam will most likely only be retained by memorization - a process which will require a great deal of concentration and practice.

Once you get the required exams out of the way, you're one step closer to officially becoming a pilot. After you get the appropriate licensing, you can work on your finances to ensure that you will be able to pay for flight school. We'll discuss the financial aspects of getting a pilot's license and becoming a private pilot in the next section.

2.3 PLAN FOR THE FINANCIAL COMPONENT OF FLIGHT SCHOOL.

Flight school can be very expensive. Flying lessons generally cost between $120 and $250 USD per hour, with the average cost being between $155 and $170 USD per hour, according to the website Lessons.com. That's why it's important to get the financial aspect under control before you begin training to ensure that you will not encounter problems paying for your training.

The cost of flight school varies based on a few factors, including the weather, and how early you can demonstrate proficiency to your instructor on each exercise. In general, you will need about $15,000 CAD, or about $11,000 USD. This amount could be less or more, depending on how fast you can make it through the coursework, your level of commitment, your relationship with your instructor, the weather, and your financial situation.

2.4 HOW DOES THE BILLING WORK?

Billing is determined by a device called a Hobbs meter, which typically keeps track of time the aircraft is in use by displaying hours and fractions of hours. The Hobbs meter begins when the airplane's propeller, or prop, starts to turn. The meter stops when the prop comes to a halt. To cut down on costs, you will want to do everything you can to practice essential skills when you are not flying the aircraft itself. Keeping in mind the Hobbs meter will focus you on practicing whatever you can when the propeller is not turning to save money.

Here are a few ways you can save money by practicing essential skills outside of the aircraft:

- "Chair fly" at home for 15 minutes a day. Sit in a chair, wherever you are, and practice flying maneuvers, making radio calls, saying everything you do aloud. It sounds strange, but it can help you improve your foundational skills, and help you save money as well. Practice crosswind takeoff, landing, and taxi scenarios with exaggerated rudder and aileron inputs.

Quiz yourself on practicing and speaking aloud every maneuver especially emergency recovery procedures for stalls, spins (in Canada), spiral dives, engine fire, electrical & radio failure, forced approach, etc. Speak aloud everything you do with your instructor as well - this will make it easier for your instructor to correct you when needed and you'll learn faster. Call out your speeds for takeoff, climb, cruise, flaps, approach, and it goes without saying to know your stall speeds. **Speed is your life and airspeed is king**!

- Taking a picture of the checklist and practicing going through it in your mind with a cockpit pic when you 'chair fly' is essential.

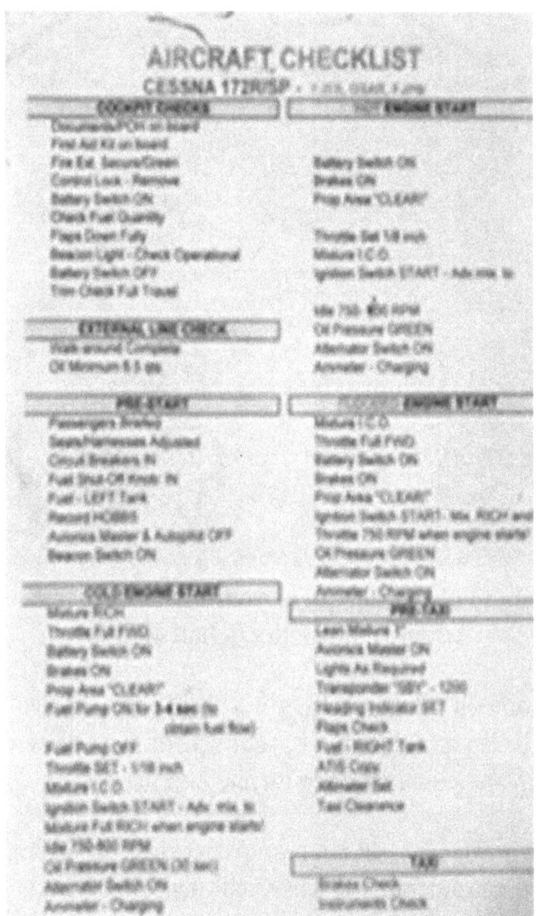

AIRCRAFT CHECKLIST

CESSNA 172R/SP

Tip: Make sure to take a picture of the aircraft checklist for 'chair flying' at home.

- Take pictures of your training aircraft's cockpit and use it to add to your chair flying while going through the checklists at home.

Tip: Take a photo of the cockpit of your aircraft for reference at home when you practice "chair flying."

- Work on all your checklists inside the airplane with the prop still. If you ask politely, your school may allow you to sit in the airplane you train on to review the checklists.

These tips will get you running your checklists faster and easier, which will save you time and money. They will also likely improve your flying abilities, which will impress your instructor.

2.5 SERIOUSLY CONSIDER GETTING EQUIPPED

Don't be afraid of enlisting technology to help you in your flight school efforts. Technology can be a great help here. Here are a few tips:

- Consider getting a small camera to take with you to your flying lessons. This way, you can record your performance, as well as your instructor's lessons and feedback, so that you can review the footage after your lesson. It can be difficult to try to absorb information during a flying lesson, so it can be useful to review afterwards.

  To do this, you will need to get a Go Pro or a similar camera to mount on your head. You will need a special adaptor to plug the head-mounted Go-Pro into the communications for this to work. Installation is straightforward: simply unplug your headset from the phone jack, plug the Go Pro cable into the phone jack, and plug your headset into the other end of the Go Pro cable. (YouTube provides an easy-to-follow instructional video by Adventure Rig.) Reviewing the footage is a great way to absorb what the instructor is saying. You will be so overwhelmed with information during flying that reviewing the flight afterwards is a great way to improve information and knowledge retention.

- Buying a handheld radio is a good idea. Having a handheld radio is a great way of being safe, as a backup communication method in case your on-board radios fail - which is, admittedly, unlikely. The main reason you would want to get a handheld radio is that, importantly, at the airport, you can listen to the ground and tower operations, and mimic the calls out loud. This practice will greatly improve your radio calls. Arrive 15 minutes early to every lesson and listen to, and mimic, the radio calls. Do not transmit so as not to interfere with air traffic operations. This will help you be the best pilot you can be by helping you familiarize yourself with the radio calls.
- Invest in a high-quality headset. This will help you cut down on costs related to your training. You can rent a headset, but this costs money over time and is unsanitary as you will likely share the rented headset with other flight students.

Having your own headset is a must, and you should opt for one that is top-of-the-line. A high-quality headset will help you perform better in your flight school training. The perfect headset will be comfortable and help you hear transmissions clearly, or you will feel uneasy, especially when you are solo. Get a used noise-cancelling headset on eBay and replace the ear and mouth cushions. You will be glad you did.

2.6 SHARPEN YOUR RADIO CALLS EARLY AND FAST.

As a pilot, you will use radio calls to communicate with Ground and Air Traffic Control (ATC). The main reason for these radio calls is that ATC &

Ground exist to help you maintain traffic separation. That's why you should work to quickly become proficient in these radio calls so that they become second nature. Communicating effectively over radio will help you significantly with issues of safety when it comes to traffic and navigation during, for example, takeoffs and landings.

The process of making radio calls may intimidate you at first. It can be difficult to effectively communicate with ATC and/or Ground as a novice. Remember, though, that everyone has to start somewhere. There are some easy ways you can work on improving your radio call skills. Here are a few tips:

- If you do not understand radio communication, you can say "repeat last" to request that the communication be stated again.
- If you do not know what you are supposed to do, you can say "request instructions for (your call sign)."
- In general, it is a good idea to take a moment to think about what you are going to say before you say it. Take a deep breath, and then transmit calmly and precisely.
- Keep it simple — focus on making your radio calls short.
- Another way to improve your radio calls is to practice at home. Spending some time each day practicing radio calls will help you be better prepared to make these calls when you are flying.

Here is an example of a concise and effective radio call:

General Radio Call (with Tower, for call sign Golf Uniform Oscar Bravo aka GUOB):

You: (After start-up checks) (*airport name*). "Ground, Golf Uniform Oscar Bravo with information Alpha"

ATC: "Golf Uniform Oscar Bravo, ground, squawk 4526 state intentions:

You: Squawk 4526, Golf Uniform Oscar Bravo at hangar 1, looking for taxi instructions to the active for (*circuits, or local flight to...*)"

ATC: "Golf Uniform Oscar Bravo taxi Alpha, hold short runway zero eight." (Everything else you write down but you must repeat back a 'hold short' restriction).

You: "Taxi Alpha, hold short 08 for Golf Uniform Oscar Bravo."

You: "(After run-up checks switch to tower frequency). (Airport name) tower: Golf Uniform Oscar Bravo holding short 08 ready for departure.”

ATC: “Golf Uniform Oscar Bravo line up and wait” or “clear for takeoff.”

You: “Line up and wait” or “clear for takeoff for Golf Uniform Oscar Bravo.”

Example For circuits

You: “Tower, Golf Uniform Oscar Bravo turning left base for runway 08 touch and go.”

Example For local flight return

You: “Tower, Golf Uniform Oscar Bravo with information Bravo.”

ATC: “Golf Uniform Oscar Bravo go ahead.”

You: “Golf Uniform Oscar Bravo 5 miles east of the field at two thousand, inbound full stop.”

ATC: “Golf Uniform Oscar Bravo cleared for landing.”

You: “Golf Uniform Oscar Bravo cleared for landing: wind check.”

ATC: “Wind 090 at 10.”

You: “Golf Uniform Oscar Bravo.”

At Touchdown

ATC: “Golf Uniform Oscar Bravo exit taxi Fox and contact Ground 121.7”. *(Note: ground frequencies always start with 121).*

You: “Fox and point seven for Golf Uniform Oscar Bravo” change to ground frequency “(airport name) ground, Golf Uniform Oscar Bravo at Fox for hanger 1” *(or say: “looking for taxi instructions back to the ramp”).*

Note: If you are unfamiliar with the airport, you can say “requesting progressive taxi instructions” *(this tells Ground you want to be led step by step where to go - don’t forget to say your call sign).*

You must practice for a few minutes aloud every day to avoid shying away from the radio, which can result in you extending your learning. That will end up costing you more money, so it’s best to practice at home, both for your wallet and your flight school success.

3.1 CHOOSE YOUR INSTRUCTOR WITH CARE

According to a 2010 study by the Aircraft Owners and Pilots Association (AOPA), about 60% of student pilots do not end up getting certified as pilots. Having a good instructor can play a large role in your success in obtaining pilot certification.

There are certain factors you should take into account in choosing your instructor for the best flight school experience. For example, a 2010 study published in *The Journal of Ergonomics* found that there is a significant increase in the effectiveness of pilot training and a significant decrease in student stress when the instructor and student have common personality types[1].

Piloting lessons – both in terms of actually flying, and answering knowledge questions related to flying - can cause a lot of anxiety. This is why it is incredibly important to choose a flight instructor who you feel safe with and who you can comfortably get along with.

Learning to fly is a commitment. You want to find an instructor who is going to be with you from the first lesson through your licensing. Having to find, or being handed off to another instructor during your piloting education will likely cause a disruption in your learning as you will have to learn how to get used to a different person – and one who you may not have chosen. So, again, you need to find an instructor who will walk with you through the entire piloting syllabus.

Again, flying can be very stressful, especially in the beginning when you are just starting to get comfortable in the airplane and with flying. In order to find an instructor who you will be able to feel comfortable and safe with and who you get along with, you will need to carefully and respectfully interview instructors from your ground school.

Make sure that the instructor you choose will be working for you and in your best interests. When approaching instructors, be respectful of their time and expertise. Above all, be respectful to the prospective instructors that you talk to.

When interviewing instructors, you will want to focus on three questions that will give you insight into who they are, their instruction style, and whether you will be compatible. You will want to ask them the following questions:

a. What are your career goals?

Ask a prospective instructor regarding their career goals in order to determine whether they're a good fit for the duration of your student pilot training. The key point of this question is to make sure that this instructor will be with the school, and available to teach you for the duration of your piloting education, — so, about two years. If they do not plan on being with the school or continuing as an instructor for at least two years, you will need to thank them for their time and respectfully move on to the next option.

b. Who is the ideal student that you would like to teach? Can you please elaborate on your ideal student's characteristics?

This and the next are the key questions that will help you determine if you and this instructor will get along well during pilot training. You want to make sure that the instructor describes someone who shares many, ideally all, of your personality traits and learning habits. If this instructor does not work well with someone with your individual personality and learning style, pilot training with them could be more stressful than it needs to be.

So, if their ideal student does not generally describe you as a student, they may have trouble teaching you effectively and you may have trouble learning from them. Either way, this will not be a valuable or enjoyable learning experience. In the case that their ideal student and your nature as a student to not align, graciously thank them for their time and respectfully move on to the next candidate.

c. How do you describe your teaching style?

This is the other side of the last question. The last question focused on whether you would be a good fit for the instructor. This question focuses specifically on whether the instructor will be a good fit for you. Does this instructor meet many or all of the characteristics you associate with your "ideal" piloting instructor? The purpose of this guide is to help you maximize what you get out of pilot training and to move through the process efficiently. This question is the most important question to make sure that you will learn as much as you can, as efficiently as possible. For this reason, you need to choose an instructor who teaches in a way that facilitates your learning. When you find an instructor, who teaches in a way that you feel comfortable with and that you think will be effective, you have completed a major part of the groundwork to start pilot training.

Congratulations, you're ready to book your flying lessons!

3.1 BEWARE OF UNNECESSARY CHARGES AND CONTROL THEM.

As we mentioned in the previous chapter, flying lessons can be expensive. Hidden costs and unnecessary charges are always something to be mindful of, especially for something like pilot training which is already a significant financial investment. There are a few easy ways that you can trim costs, without cutting corners, while still getting the most out of your training experience.

First, you can trim the cost of the textbook "From the Ground Up" by purchasing a used copy online. Check with your instructor and/or school first, and, of course, it depends on availability of used copies online, but you will likely be able to get everything you need to know without having to shell out significant funds for a brand-new copy.

Being prepared for briefings with your instructor is another way you can save both time and money. You can avoid unnecessary charges for meetings by asking your instructor to let you know ahead of time what they want to discuss in their out-of-class briefings — these are briefings on days you are not scheduled to fly. Politely ask your instructor if you can hold the briefing at your next flying lesson on the way back to the airport. Make sure they let you know exactly what they want to discuss in their briefing so you can study these topics before your next class meeting.

If your instructor introduces any extra meetings (such as briefings) or extra preparatory equipment, make sure you ask and fully understand the cost before you agree.

You can save significant money and time by being proactive about studying. Knowing what information or skills you need and finding ways to study and practice these outside of class meetings is a relatively simple way to save significant money. You can find books, internet How-To guides, or YouTube videos that can offer you instruction on basic requirements such as learning how to interpret the Terminal Aerodrome Forecast (TAF) and Meteorological Terminal Air Report (METAR). You will also want to use

YouTube videos to become very familiar with the ATIS Weather report and what it means. This will help you move through your training more quickly and avoid the need for extra meetings or lessons.

Another cost-saving tip is to skip the "Fam (Familiarization) Flight." This is meant for entertainment purposes only and is not a necessary or skill-building exercise.

3.2 BASIC PLANNING

Once you have decided to become a pilot, before you decide who you want as your instructor, the first question to think about is where you want to attend flight school. There are four key questions you want to ask yourself. You will need to weigh the importance of each of these factors – deciding which is more important – in order to decide where you will attend your flight classes:

> a. How far am I willing to travel to attend flight school (flying classes)?
> b. How important is it that I go to my top preferred school?
> c. How important is it that I get to learn with my top preferred instructor?
> d. How important is it that I go to a school near my home?

Your flight school and your instructor should show an appreciation for your time and expense and should be working to make your money worth it. Also, presumably, you do not want to have to repeat this process, so it is of paramount importance to make sure that you are getting the most out of your flight school experience. But you also don't want to make flight school so difficult to attend (i.e. so far away) that you are disincentivized from attending your classes. Ultimately you will need to decide what factors are going to give you the most valuable and achievable experience.

Once you have decided on your flight school and instructor you will want to make sure you have a crystal-clear understanding of the requirements for flight school. You want to make sure you fully understand the syllabus requirements as well as the lessons involved and in what order they will occur. You will want to understand how these requirements vary based on the weather and what affect the weather will have on your ability to complete your flight classes. You will need to understand the impact of weather on your lessons both before and after your first solo flight.

You will want to think ahead to when you will begin your lessons. You would do well to time your training so that you can take advantage of daylight savings time. You will also want to look ahead at the weather and think about the time of year so that you can optimize your lessons by taking advantage of favorable weather when you schedule your lessons.

In order to get the most out of your experience and to move through flight school in a timely manner, you need to be ready to immerse yourself. Immersion is key to honing strong and second nature flying skills. Leaving too much time in between lessons means leaving time for your brain and muscles to forget what you learned in your last lesson. You will want to be ready to fly at least 3 times per week if you are still working on preparing for your exams. However, it is ideal to finish your exams first so that you can focus solely on flying lessons. If your exams are finished, you will have more free time to work on flying, so you should be flying four times per week.

4.1 Choose Your Airplane for the Long Term

You will want to choose the airplane in which you conduct flight lessons carefully. Think long-term, and consider what factors are important to you in renting an aircraft. You have some choices, including the Cessna Model 150/152, the popular Cessna 172 Skyhawk (C172), the Piper PA-28 Cherokee, and American Champion Citabria. These four aircrafts are commonly considered the easiest to learn to fly in.

4.2 Evaluate Your Options

Cessna Model 150/152

The Cessna 150 is a two-seated airplane designed for flight training, touring, and personal use. It is the fifth most produced civilian plane ever, with nearly 24,000 airplanes produced. Developed starting in the 1950s, the Model 150 uses a tricycle landing gear, which is more intuitive to learn how to use than previous landing gears. Production of the Model 150 halted in 1977, as the aircraft was phased out in favor of the newer Model 152.

1970 Cessna FA150K (G-AYCF) landing at Hullavington airfield, Wiltshire,

England. Built 1970. Source: Wikipedia.

CESSNA 172 SKYHAWK

The Cessna 172 Skyhawk is one of the most popular single-engine aircrafts ever and a good choice for aviation training. More 172s have been built than any other aircraft. Manufacturing of the 172 Skyhawk started in 1955, and the aircraft is still in production, with over 44,000 units being built to date. With four seats, a single engine, and high, fixed wings, the Cessna 172 is larger than the Model 150 and has a few other improved flying characteristics. In particular, the 172 Skyhawk boasts great visibility, an advanced glass cockpit, slow landing speed, and a forgiving stall.

1960 Cessna 172A. Source: Wikipedia.

PIPER PA-28 CHEROKEE LINE

The Piper PA-28 Cherokee line of popular training planes include the Warrior (a particularly popular choice for student pilots), the Arrow, the Acher TX and LX, and the Pilot 100 and i100.This line of 2-4 seat light aircraft compete with the Cessna 172 and are designed for flight training, air taxiing, and personal use. These planes are all metal, unpressurized, piston-powered, with a single-engine, low-mounted wings, and tricycle landing gear. The Piper line was first introduced in 1960 and has been in continuous production since 1961. Models range in engine size from 140 to 300 hp. Some models include retractable gear and constant speed propellers. The

Piper PA-28 line is designed to compete with the Cessna 172 by offering lower manufacturing and parts costs.

Piper Warrior II. Source: Wikipedia

AMERICAN CHAMPION CITABRIA

The American Champion Citabria is a line of single engine, 2-seater, light aircraft and sport plane. These planes have fixed conventional gear. The Citabria line was first introduced in 1964 and has been in production since, now offering five models. These planes are designed for flight training, utility, and personal use. The key distinctive feature of these planes is their ability to sustain aerobatic stresses from +5g to -2g.

American Champion Citabria. Source: Wikipedia

WEIGH THE PROS AND CONS OF DIFFERENT AIRCRAFTS

The 150 is cheaper to rent. But the C172 is a little easier to learn on and to control in windy conditions, and, with a maximum occupancy of four people, obviously passenger-friendly in the long term.

If you are a little sensitive to air sickness, I suggest learning on the slightly more expensive Cessna 172 R&S, which uses a fuel injection engine, to help make the quality of your experience a little smoother and more positive. Using a plane with fuel injection means that you don't have to worry about managing carburetor heat — which is one less thing for you to do.

Another important aspect to consider when choosing a plane is wing configuration. This refers to the placement of the wings in relation to the fuselage — or body, of the plane. High wings mean that the wings are positioned on top of the plane's fuselage. Mid wing airplanes have wings positioned at the midline of the plane's fuselage. Finally, low wings are positioned below the fuselage midline.

Wing configuration affects the stability and maneuverability of a plane as well as external visibility from within the plane. High wing planes are the most stable, particularly at low speeds, meaning they will react more quickly to adjustments during turbulence. However, high wing planes have the least upward external visibility from within the plane.

Mid wing planes are very balanced due to the large amount of control surface and are very maneuverable but less stable than high wing planes. Mid wing plane external visibility is better than that from within high wing planes, but not as good as low wing planes.

Low wing planes are more stable than mid wing planes but less stable than those with high wings but are more maneuverable than high wing planes. Low wing planes offer the best visibility from within the plane.

The number of seats (the size) of a plane also affects plane handling. Four seat planes are easier to handle than two seaters. However, four seater planes are more expensive.

Whatever you choose, find a particular airplane you like and stick to it whenever possible. This will make your radio calls and internal cockpit focus easier, since the name of the airplane, and its cockpit layout, will not change.

CHAPTER 5:

5.1 GET YOUR MIND RIGHT

Having the right mindset is essential to flying. Too much stress and anxiety can affect your ability to make decisions, which can be dangerous in the cockpit.

Remember that the airplane is not a classroom — you learn faster, and in a more cost-effective manner, when you stimulate and stretch your understanding of the material when you are on the ground. Therefore, when the prop is turning, you are merely proving to yourself and your instructor what you know.

Stay relaxed when flying, studying, and figuring-out unforeseen challenges that may pop up as you learn.

Take many moments along the way to **enjoy this new experience**, and take pride in all of the skills you are acquiring that most people will never have.

Be patient with yourself. As with anything, there are several learning curves in flying, because you are learning new skills and habits and pursuing new experiences. Expect that you will make mistakes, and that you will have to take a step back before proceeding forward with your learning many times — both on paper and in the airplane.

Focus on understanding, not memorizing. Expect that it may take you a little longer to understand the material completely — this will allow the information to imprint itself into your mind so you can recall it when it counts — because one day it may.

Practice consequential thinking to show yourself and your instructor you understand the material deeply. Consequential thinking involves both critical thinking and emotional intelligence, and can help us have confidence in our inherent abilities while rendering us able to overcome and deal with our emotions. Good decision-making is crucial in the cockpit and so consequential thinking can be useful to assess choices, anticipate how people will react, and follow intentions.

Here's some advice to improve your consequential thinking in and outside of the aircraft:

- You will be asked in briefings before flights what you would do in certain emergencies that you have already studied. Your answers should follow a calm, logical flow. Provide reasons for your anticipated actions in these situations, so that the emergency situations you are dealing with in these hypothetical scenarios do not become worse.

For example, with an engine fire, the first thing to do is to stop pumping fuel out to the fire. So, your response might be something like, "I'd cut the mixture and turn off the fuel tanks. I would keep flying and move on to the 2nd procedure," and so on.

- Fully commit to getting your pilot's license with no plan B in case of failure. Your plan B will only interfere with plan A and hold you back from the end goal of becoming a pilot. Your plan A is to get your pilot's licence. Hesitation will only hold you back, and slow your progress and cost you more time, and therefore, more money.

5.2 MAINTAIN SITUATIONAL AWARENESS AT ALL TIMES

It is important to maintain situational awareness at all times when on the journey to obtaining your pilot's license. Situational awareness means being attuned to everything happening around you as well as being aware of what you are doing — having overall perception of the environmental elements with respect to time and space. The periodical *Aviation Safety* offers a few suggestions to maintain proper situational awareness.

- **Think ahead.** Think about where the airplane will be in a few minutes from now, and what will happen when the aircraft reaches decision altitude.
- **Be vigilant.** Look for anything that could pose a risk to your flight. Think about how others may react when you respond to threats.
- **Go with your gut feeling.** Sometimes we may be inclined to ignore our gut feelings. Don't. Approach flying with a cautious and doubtful attitude, and make sure to verify your perceptions before responding.
- **Avoid overload.** Don't do too much at once, or you risk doing all of them poorly. Prioritize tasks, if you can, and address them

one-by-one.
- **Make sure you are well-rested.** Modify your sleep-wake cycle to make sure that you will get enough sleep before your flight.
- **Constantly assess the situation.** Circumstances are bound to change. Whether relating to weather, equipment status, fuel, or traffic, make sure that you stay apprised of the situation so that you can make changes to your plans as needed.

It is important to maintain situational awareness at all times when on the journey to obtaining your pilot's license. Situational awareness means being attuned to everything happening around you — having overall perception of the environmental elements with respect to time and space.

The big-picture value of situational awareness is that it allows you to pre-empt and immediately respond to issues that arise during flight. In other words, situational awareness is about "predicting the future." Of course, you're not expected to be a psychic, but you should be paying attention to what's happening in and outside of the airplane and using your experience, knowledge, and reasoning to remain aware of potential difficulties. You need to be aware of where the plane is and where it's going as well as what you might encounter when you get there. You need to think ahead to changes in the environment within and outside of the airplane and what changes could occur to the plane's functioning. In short, you need to be aware of and prepared for any potential threats that could arise. This is a lot of information and part of this awareness will likely be on the subconscious level so trust your intuition. If something feels off, investigate it.

In terms of your mental state and behaviors that promote or diminish situational awareness, you need to manage the amount of activities that demand your attention. In order to reserve as much of your attention as possible for situational awareness, try to minimize the amount of activities you are engaging in. That is, focus on one task at a time. Similarly, another way to minimize the risk of task or information overload is to take precautionary and in-flight steps to avoid fatigue. Finally, in terms of optimizing your capacity to stay truly aware of your surroundings and potential threats, you should maintain a healthy sense of fear – that is, don't ever become comfortable to the point that you go on "auto pilot." Situational awareness takes a great deal of mental energy and needs to be maintained from the moment you start the engine to the moment you come to a full stop!

During your training, focus on showing yourself and your instructor that, while you are in flight, you are working towards calmly knowing what you are doing, where you are, where you are going, and what is happening both inside and outside the cockpit. *Flight Literacy* states that situational awareness centers on awareness of "all the factors and conditions within the five fundamental risk elements (flight, pilot, aircraft, environment, and type of operation that comprise any given aviation situation)." **Say aloud everything you do and what you are going to do**. This will help put you and the instructor at ease, and you will have a better experience.

Every flight school and/or flight instructor has their own preference for shorthand methods for learning to instill and practice situational awareness. One example of a relatively straightforward method to prepare yourself to practice situational awareness during steep turns, stalls, and slow flight maneuvers is to work through the acronym HASEL. The HASEL method is one of many easy to remember and implement methods of learning and practicing situational awareness:

Height (are you at a safe and legal altitude)

Area (If in an emergency where can you make a forced approach landing, and where is the wind blowing, or what was the last known surface and upper wind report)

Safety (seatbelts, windows, breathe deep, passenger comfort check)

Engine (check all guages quickly and efficiently - priority is looking outside the airplane)

Lookout (maintain a listening watch on the radio, lookout for traffic avoidance and know where you are going)

Once you have learned the HASEL method by heart and can incorporate it naturally you can begin to practice the shorter version for maintaining situational awareness by priority:

1. Aviate: never stop flying the airplane by panicking
2. Navigate: know where you want to go, where you are going and where you have been and your speed
3. Communicate: never hesitate to call ATC or flight following for help if you are lost

5.3 Look to the greats of aviation to develop the right mindset.

What do famous pilots say about good piloting? Here are a few best-practice trainings and learning quotes from famous aviation icons that can help you get in the right frame of mind:

"Fighter pilots have ice in their veins. They don't have emotions. They think and anticipate. They know that fear and other concerns cloud your mind from what's going on and what you should be involved in."

– NASA Astronaut Buzz Aldrin,
second man to walk on the moon

"Learning to fly an airplane taught me a way of thinking, an approach to problem-solving that was applicable and effective. Pilots are very methodical and meticulous, and artists tend not to be."

– Chris Carter,
pilot and flight instructor

"I have often been asked what I think about at the moment of take-off. Of course, no pilot sits and feels his pulse as he flies. He has to be part of the machine. If he thinks of anything but the task in hand, then trouble is probably just around the corner."

– Amelia Earhart,
first female aviator to fly solo across the Atlantic Ocean

"Being a 'good stick' is not enough. Good pilots are thinking their way through the air as well as simply moving controls. What comes next in flight is absolutely as important as what is happening right now."

– Jack J. Pelton,
former CEO of Cessna Aircraft Company

"Flying an airplane is a challenge. It tests you personally. It tests your limits. You learn more about yourself being a pilot than anything else."

– Michael Goulian,
multi-disciplined aerial demonstration pilot.

"A true aviator really sees aviation as a whole, constantly improving but while still being humble, and realizing that you can never know everything there is to know."

– Patty Wagstaff,
pilot and flight instructor

"You do what you can for as long as you can, and when you finally can't, you do the next best thing. You back up but you don't give up."

– Chuck Yeager,
first pilot to break the sound barrier

"You don't concentrate on risks. You concentrate on results. No risk is too great to prevent the necessary job from getting done."

– Chuck Yeager,
first pilot to break the sound barrier

"We have all heard about ordinary people who find themselves in extraordinary situations. They act courageously or responsibly, and their efforts are described as if they opted to act that way on the spur of the moment... I believe many people in those situations actually have made decisions years before."

– Capt. Chesley "Sully" Sullenberger,
heroic "Miracle on the Hudson" pilot

"In so many areas of life, you need to be a long-term optimist but a short-term realist."

– Capt. Chesley "Sully" Sullenberger,
heroic "Miracle on the Hudson" pilot

"What kind of man would live where there is no daring? I don't believe in taking foolish chances, but nothing can be accomplished without taking any chance at all."

– Charles Lindbergh,
pilot who made the first solo transatlantic airplane flight

"Once you have learned to fly your plane, it is far less fatiguing to fly than it is to drive a car. You don't have to watch every second for cats, dogs, children, lights, road signs, ladies with baby carriages and citizens who drive out in the middle of the block against the lights. Nobody who has not been up in the sky on a glorious morning can possibly imagine the way a pilot feels in free heaven."

– William T. Piper,
founder of Piper Aircraft Corporation

"A good pilot constantly decodes the raw data the airplane is communicating into consumable information quickly and easily."
– Col. Tim Duffy,
September 11th F15 Fighter Pilot

"It is possible to fly without motors, but not without knowledge and skill."
– Wilbur Wright,
inventor of modern flight

"Never interrupt someone doing what you said couldn't be done."
– Amelia Earhart,
first female aviator to fly solo across the Atlantic Ocean

"Don't ever let a fear of failing keep you from knowing the joys of flight."
– Lane Wallace,
aviation author and journalist

"Great pilots are made, not born. A man may possess good eyesight, sensitive hands, and perfect coordination, but the end result is only fashioned by steady coaching, much practice, and experience."
– James Edgar Johnson,
Air Vice-Marshal of the British Royal Air Force

5.4 Student pilot best practices

Learning to fly is expensive, time-consuming, and challenging, but it can also be one of the most rewarding and exciting experiences you will ever have. The key to getting the most out of your experience: making the most of your time and money - and making sure you are successful is to maintain best practices from the start. Best practices can be categorized into three areas that correspond to different aspects of the flight training experience: preparation, practice, and mindset.

Be prepared! A key to getting the most out of your flight school experience and specifically your flight training is to make sure you come ready to fly. This includes maintaining your physical health by making sure that you are well rested and that you are eating well as well as maintaining your emotional health by making sure you are working to reduce stress and avoiding information-overload. It also means making sure that you have the knowledge you need before you get in the air. A good rule is to *learn on the ground and practice in the air*. This means knowing your learning objectives and making sure to use each flight to meet them, passing the written exams before flying, knowing your plane, and using pre/post flight briefings to maximize your learning experience. Lastly, remember to stay curious! Always seek out what you don't know and make it your mission to learn it.

Practice! Practice! Practice! It is said that it takes 10,000 hours to master a skill. While there is no short-cutting this time frame, there are ways to make sure you get the most out of your practice and to make sure you don't have to invest *more* time than this. The most important thing you can do is fly as often as possible. The 10,000 hour rule refers to the amount of time it takes to gain enough experience and muscle memory that the skill becomes "second-nature." Flight simulators are an excellent way to practice procedures without having to rent a plane or pay an instructor, using simulators are the next best thing to flying and will save you significant expense. Making sure to maintain diversity in your flight training objectives will not only help you learn new skills but it will also help you maintain the skills you have - remember, just because you "passed" in an area of training does not mean you don't have to keep practicing this skill. Finally, finding a mentor is one of the best ways to make sure you get the most out of your practice - your mentor can provide you with invaluable advice and access to the lessons they have learned through their own experience.

Perception is 90% of reality. The final key to making sure you have the most productive, successful, and enjoyable flight training experience is to keep the right mindset. Remember to <u>stay focused on staying one step ahead</u> : the cockpit is noisy and cramped and it can be difficult to learn in this kind of environment, but staying focused will help ensure that you do not freeze up or miss valuable learning opportunities. Stay confident in your ability to learn - without becoming overconfident in your skills. Also remember that setbacks and frustrations are unavoidable - learning any new skill requires trial and error and repetition - you will make mistakes and you will not master the skill in the first try, the key is to stay emotionally resilient, maintain your ambition, and bounce back. It is important that you communicate your feelings, concerns, and struggles openly with your flight instructor, both for your own stress levels and to ensure that you are learning everything you need to know. Equally important is practicing continual self-assessment, which means maintaining a clear picture of your habits and your learning process. One last key to mindset is to <u>live what you do</u>: don't just practice flying, become a pilot in identity and community.

Here are a few best practices you should follow for the actual flying component of pilot school — not for exams, but for your first solo circuit and solo cross-country flight.

6.1 BASIC HANDLING

PERFECT YOUR CIRCUIT PATTERNS

Perfect circuit patterns – otherwise referred to as airfield traffic patterns — are integral to safe flying and the first step in a perfect landing. Perfecting your speed control is key for perfecting your circuit patterns.

Circuit patterns follow a standardized design to maintain safety and traffic separation around the airport and to control noise pollution in nearby residential areas. To maintain a safe distance from other planes in a pilot-controlled airspace, you must anticipate the next leg position in the pattern. This requires clear radio calls, keeping a mental picture of the surrounding airplanes in the pattern, as well as maintaining precise speeds for takeoff, cruise, flaps, and the final approach. By using the pitch control in each leg position, you can stay ahead of the airplane's tendency to meander without your inputs.

Further, circuit patterns are the first step in the landing process. A perfected circuit pattern – and speed control, will set you up for a safe and smooth landing.

PERFECT YOUR LANDINGS

At the beginning bumpy landings will be inevitable. Learning how to land safely and comfortably will take time and will likely be one of the more challenging of the routine aspects of flying that you will need to learn. However, following these steps in the landing process can exponentially increase your comfort with landings:

1. Aim to land your plane on the runway numbers. Do not force it. Keep the wings level and maintain control. When encountering a crosswind, you will need to adjust your inputs and power to align the airplane with the runway and maintain control over your sink rate. You will need to maintain your inputs until touchdown in order to land smoothly.

2. **Flare** – transition into slow flight, when the runway appears to

fill the sides of the windshield

Knowing when to start your flare to pull back and transition into slow flight is essential. It may help you to use this scene in your mind as a visual cue to start and maintain your flare.

3. At this stage, take your eyes all the way down the runway until touchdown while maintaining backpressure on the yoke.

4. At the same time, stay busy on the rudder, making minor corrections as needed to stay on the centreline. In a crosswind, once you have landed, remember your crosswind taxi techniques until shut down.

Following these steps will significantly improve your handling and confidence in landings. The more comfortable you become with each step in the landing process, the better you will become at anticipating each step and preparing for any issues. Anticipation and preparation are key to safe and smooth flying. Instinctive knowledge of each step of the process – whether circuit patterns, take-offs, or landings – will allow you the mental space for anticipation of and preparation for any special circumstances.

Utilizing your time with your instructor to practice airplane handling for different practice-landing techniques is an excellent way to build knowledge and comfort with landing in the safety of a "learning" " environment. Two key techniques to ask your instructor to work with you on are "low and overs" down the runway and "slow flight down the runway."

Practicing "low and overs" down the runway is a great way to practice maintaining speed, altitude, and runway position (centering). This technique will get you used to the feeling of floating in ground-effect during the landing process.

Running through "slow flight down the runway" with your instructor will give you an opportunity to practice rudder control and corrections during the landing process. While you are practicing this technique, you will need to focus on making minor and gentle rudder corrections to best align your longitudinal axis to the runway centreline. You will also want to ask your instructor to demonstrate, then let you practice this technique in moderate crosswind conditions to make sure that you are prepared to handle the plane during landing in different wind conditions.

Practice these techniques until the process is instinctive and you are able to anticipate and prepare for any possible contingencies and correct for any weather conditions. This will significantly improve your confidence by building your skills in handling the airplane expertly to provide safe and smooth landings. This skill and confidence will make you a safer pilot and your future passengers will feel they can trust you when the landings are gentle.

6.2 CREATE FAST TRACK LEARNING PRIORITIES

When preparing for your solo flight you want to focus on the key learning priorities. The best way to do this is to create a schedule of fast-track learning priorities. Setting these priorities and sticking to a schedule for learning them will help keep you focused on each individual task. This step-by-step focus will keep you on track by allowing you to identify each key concept in a clear and simplified way. Below are some of the most important things you will need to know in order to have a safe, smooth, and fun solo flight.

Where You're Going and How You're Getting There

One of the most basic things you will need to know to prepare for your first solo cross-country flight is the details of the flight:

- How long will the flight be?

- How much fuel will be required plus weight and balance?
- Where will you be departing?
- Where and how will you be landing?
- What route are you taking?
- What kind of weather do you expect along the route?
- What sites for air traffic control and obstructions will there be along the route?
- What are the current legal airspace requirements for departure, enroute, and destination?
- Where, enroute, could you make an emergency landing?
- Don't forget to take the journey log for maintenance reference if repairs were ever needed

Situational Awareness, continued...

You will also need to make sure that you have anticipated and prepared for any weather related contingency. Review your manual and practice course- corrections in the case of unforeseen inclement weather conditions. Use the techniques discussed in Section 5.2 on Situational Awareness to practice thinking and acting aloud. You can practice this at home, in a simulated flight, or with your instructor. Review the situations that require waiting out take-offs or landings during inclement weather or runway conditions.

Air Traffic Control Communications

Make sure you have an intuitive grasp on air traffic control communications and frequencies. Test your air communications procedures alone and with your instructor. Practice communications under a variety of circumstances and for various points in your flight (take off, in air, landing) to ensure that you will be able to communicate effectively when you need to during your solo flight. Knowing how and when to use ATC's "flight following" instruction – to allow ATC to track your plane and know where it is in reference to other air traffic, is a valuable tool and would be the first resource in case of an emergency, but it is encouraged to contact "flight following" on any destination flight.

Obviously, knowing how to fly the plane: perfecting take-offs, airborne flying, and landings, provides the basis of necessary knowledge for your solo flight. However, as you've just read, there are other equally important factors and processes that you will need to have a deep understanding of before you can expect your instructor to endorse your first or cross-country solo.

6.3 UTILIZE YOUTUBE TUTORIALS

- Look to YouTube for help to learn about essential concepts such as:

    - E6B Flight Computer Usage
    - Calculations for: crosswind component, weight & balance, cross-country legs
    - How to read and interpret flight charts

YouTube is an excellent resource for learning about essential concepts and skills. Tutorials provide you with accessible guides to learning. Video logs (vlogs) provide you with valuable insight into the actual experiences of other students and instructors. Since most tutorials should be providing you with the same basic information, the key is to choose tutorial videos that will teach you in the most effective way — that is, choose the tutorial that matches your learning style.

YouTube tutorials are most beneficial when you want to understand a concept, its background, its relationship to other concepts, and its application, as well as when you want to learn certain skills such as calculating weight and balance or how to read flight charts.

YouTube vlogs are most beneficial when you want to hear about other students' and instructors' experiences during flight school, examinations, and solo flights to gain an impression of what it feels like to be a flight student in different scenarios.

Here are some examples of the multitude of YouTube tutorials and vlogs that are available:

E6B Flight Computer – Manual (or Graphic) Tutorial
YouTube: E6B Flight Computer: Time, Speed, & Distance by MzeroA Flight Training
YouTube: How to Use an E6B Flight Computer by Flying Mentor

E6B Flight Computer – Digital (or Electronic) Tutorial

YouTube: How to Use Sporty's Electronic E6B Flight Computer by Sporty's Pilot Shop

Calculating Crosswind Component Tutorial:
YouTube: Crosswind Component Chart (Private Pilot Lesson 7b) by Cyndy Hollman
YouTube: Pilot Mental Math: Crosswind Component by 74 Gear

Calculating Weight and Balance Tutorial:
YouTube: Calculating Weight and Balance by MzeroA Flight Training
YouTube: Weight and Balance Calculations (Private Pilot Lesson 1g) by Cyndy Hollman

Calculating Cross-Country Legs Tutorial:
YouTube: Cross Country Flight Planning by MzeroA Flight Training
YouTube: Determining Top of Climb for Cross Country Flight for Student Pilots by Part Time Pilot

How to Read Flight Charts Tutorial:
YouTube: How to Read a VFR Sectional Chart by MzeroA Flight Training
YouTube: Ep. 34: How to Read a VFR Sectional Chart (Basic Chart/Map Knowledge) by FLY8MA.com Flight Training

Solo Flight Vlogs:
YouTube: My First Solo Flight by Pure Living for Life
YouTube: My First Solo Flight PPL Student with Commentary from Duxford UK by TimesWithJames

6.4 PREPARING FOR YOUR CHECKRIDE

The Checkride is the final practical examination of your piloting skills and academic knowledge intermixed with your ability to make sound judgements, to practice consequential thinking, and to prioritize and maintain safety. You will be expected to answer exam questions both on the ground before take-off and while in the air.

Your Checkride examiner will be analyzing your responses on both accuracy and conciseness. You want to offer the most fully accurate answers possible in the briefest way possible. Nervousness is inevitable and expected, but you will need to focus on not expressing that nervous energy through overly wordy or convoluted explanations.

During this exam you will need to prove to your examiner that you can apply your technical and academic knowledge in the safest way to skillfully handle yourself and your plane and resolve any issues in various unusual scenarios. Your examiner is not your enemy — they want to see you succeed, but they also have a responsibility to ensure the safety of you and all other pilots and passengers by analyzing your explanations for the decisions you make or would make to find and test your weaknesses as a pilot. It is the examiner's job to assess your weaknesses and the safety issues they may present.

Reading your Pilot Operating Handbook cover to cover and learning all of the material well enough to know when to apply it and how to accurately and concisely explain it when asked by the instructor is key to success in your Checkride exam. YouTube vlogs and tutorials about the Checkride exam are another great resource to prepare you for this exam. These videos can give you a good idea not only of what will be expected of you in terms of knowledge and skills but can give you an impression of what it will feel like to take the exam.

Chapter 7: Concluding Remarks

Learning to fly can be an incredibly rewarding and gratifying experience. Regardless of whether you choose to get your pilot's license for business or leisurely flying, the process can be greatly simplified by relying on the advice of someone who has already been through it all.

Once again, Congratulations on considering or deciding to pursue a dream that few people will experience first-hand. Stay excited, curious and meticulous in learning all you can - once you get the flying bug - it may change how you define yourself.

It's a great day to be alive! Flight school and flying can give you a unique, birds-eye view of life — literally.

www.ingramcontent.com/pod-product-compliance
Lightning Source LLC
Chambersburg PA
CBHW020943160726
47993CB00007B/2909